Happy Hanukkah!

L'Chaim ~

Emalie
Ortega

THE LITTLE BOOK OF
JEWISH
WISDOM

THE LITTLE BOOK OF

JEWISH WISDOM

compiled by

M a r t i n   H o r a n

ELEMENT

Shaftesbury, Dorset ❖ Rockport, Massachusetts
Brisbane, Queensland

© Element Books Limited 1995
© Text compilation Martin Horan 1995

First published in Great Britain in 1995 by
ELEMENT BOOKS LIMITED
Shaftesbury, Dorset SP7 8BP

Published in the USA in 1995 by
ELEMENT BOOKS, INC.
PO Box 830, Rockport, MA 01966

Published in Australia in 1995 by
ELEMENT BOOKS LIMITED
for JACARANDA WILEY LIMITED
33 Park Road, Milton, Brisbane 4064

Designed and created by:
The Bridgewater Book Company / Jane Lanaway
Picture research by Felicity Cox
Printed in Italy by LEGO

British Library Cataloguing in Publication data available

Library of Congress Cataloging in Publication data available

ISBN 1-85230-722-6

Introduction

THE JEWS have been collecting and recording the sayings and debates of their teachers, scholars and philosophers for almost 3,000 years. We find them in the Bible as well as in the Talmud – virtual libraries (there are two Talmuds) of commentary on religion, law, philosophy and ethics that took 1,200 years to compile.

I have quoted from various books of the Bible and the Talmud as well as from the writings of rabbis, such as Hillel, Maimonides and Ben Syra, who to Jews are famous. I have also quoted from Jewish folklore – both the chasidic (ultra orthodox) and the secular, the ancient and the modern.

The Jewish imagination is highly influenced by suffering and is often the product of the ghetto, so its humour is often wry and ironical.

For balance I have included quotes from assimilated Jews, some of them renegades and apostates. Proust, for example, was not raised as a Jew but, due to his origins, is often regarded as Jewish. I would have included quotes of converts too, had I known of any who had written or said something worth recording. No doubt many have, and the Midrash says that a convert is dearer to God than a person born into the religion.

Although in such a small book space is limited, I feel I have managed to quote from all sections of Jewish life – rich and poor, the scholarly and the unlettered, the famous and the obscure – which I believe have contributed to the enrichment of our civilization. By doing so, I intend to show that wisdom comes in all shapes and guises.

MARTIN HORAN

THE PURSUIT of knowledge for its own sake, an almost fanatical love of justice, and the desire for personal independence – these are the features of the Jewish tradition which makes me thank my stars that I belong to it.

ALBERT EINSTEIN

THERE ARE three impudent creatures: among beasts, the dog; among birds, the cock; among people, Israel. But Rabbi Ammi added: 'Do not consider this as blame; it is praise, for to be a Jew means to be ready to be martyred.'

MIDRASH: *Exodus Rabbah 42:9*

THE LORD bless thee and keep thee;
The Lord make his face shine upon thee,
and be gracious unto thee.
The Lord lift up his countenance upon
thee and give thee peace.

THE BOOK OF NUMBERS 6:24–26

BE SURE your sin will find you out.

NUMBERS 32:23

THERE ARE two types of men: one
who is first rate, and fate made him last;
the other, who should be last, and fate
put him first.

MOSES IBN EZRA: *Shirat Yisroel*

𝒲HEN A man hears evil reports concerning his fellow from one person they must not be believed unless they be substantiated, then they may be believed. When a man sees anyone doing evil, he should rebuke him directly and, if necessarily, repeatedly. A pupil may rebuke his master if he thinks he will listen to him, and he should rebuke his fellow man if he will not listen to him. It is prohibited to tell others what he has heard from his fellow without his consent. One must not speak too much of his fellow's goodness, for too much praise may lead to his disgrace. A visitor must not praise his host lest too many other visitors become a burden to him.

LAWS AND CUSTOMS OF ISRAEL

*P*RAY THAT you will never have to suffer
all that you are able to endure.

FOLK SAYING

❧ ❧

*E*YES ARE like sponges; they soak
into themselves a man's
experiences, they reflect back his
ancestry and his heritage. They are
like breasts filled with the milk of
awareness. Look into a man's eyes
and – without words, without any
concrete exchange but only
through an infinite understanding –
you sense the partnership of all
mankind. You are his brother. You
understand him. You bind yourself
to him in a realization of common
brotherhood and common destiny.

SHOLEM ASCH

ALMS ARE the salt of riches.

HEBREW PROVERB

SAY LITTLE, do much, and receive all
men with a cheerful countenance.

TALMUD: *Pirke Abot*

THE HATRED of other men destroys
your own soul.

SAYINGS OF THE FATHERS 2:15

NEED MAKES people better; luck
makes them worse.

CHASIDIC SAYING

THE FEAR of the Lord is the beginning of knowledge: but fools despise wisdom and instruction.

My son, hear the instruction of thy father, and forsake not the law of thy mother:

For they shall be an ornament of grace unto thy head, and chains about thy neck.

Wisdom crieth without; she uttereth her voice in the streets:

She crieth in the chief place of concourse, in the openings of the gates: in the city she uttereth her words, saying,

How long, ye simple ones, will ye love simplicity? and the scorners delight in their scorning, and fools hate knowledge.

Turn you at my reproof: behold, I will pour out my spirit unto you, I will make known my words unto you.

Because I have called, and ye refused; I have stretched out my hand, and no man regarded;

But ye have set at nought all my counsel, and would none of my reproof:

I also will laugh at your calamity; I will mock when your fear cometh;

When your fear cometh as desolation, and your destruction cometh as a whirlwind; when distress and anguish cometh upon you.

Then they shall call upon me, but I will not answer; they shall seek me early, but they shall not find me:

For that they hated knowledge, and did not choose the fear of the Lord:

They would none of my counsel: they despised all my reproof.

Therefore shall they eat of the fruit
of their own way, and be filled with
their own devices.

For the turning away of the simple shall
slay them, and the prosperity of fools
shall destroy them.

But whoso hearken unto me shall dwell
safely, and shall be quiet from fear of evil.

THE BOOK OF PROVERBS 1:7–33

$\mathcal{T}$HE FOLLOWING are general moral rules:
not to talk about other people except
for some good cause. Neither to utter nor
to listen to idle words which serve no
useful purpose. To cultivate a silent tongue
and not to talk except to acquire wisdom
or to satisfy the needs of one's physical life.

To speak gently with one's fellow
creatures. Not to talk of material things
in the house of study. To learn from every
man and to accept the truth from all who
speak it. To be anxious to promote the
welfare of his fellow and to pursue peace.

To remember the day of death and
continually to have in one's mind the
purpose of his creation in this world.

LAWS AND CUSTOMS OF ISRAEL

*B*ETTER ASK ten times than go
astray once.

YIDDISH PROVERB

❦

*W*HAT NATURE delivers to us is never
stale. Because what nature creates has
eternity in it.

ISAAC BASHEVIS SINGER

*B*Y THREE things is the world sustained:
by justice, by truth and by peace.

THE TALMUD: *Pirke Abot*

❦

*O*NE MUST not cheat anybody, not even
in the world of one's triumph.

FRANZ KAFKA

...Naked I came out of my mother's womb, and naked shall I return thither: the Lord gave, and the Lord hath taken away; blessed be the name of the Lord.

...So went Satan forth from the presence of the Lord, and smote Job with sore boils from the sole of his foot unto his crown.

And he took him a potsherd to scrape himself withal; and he sat down among the ashes.

Then said his wife unto him, Dost thou still retain thine integrity? curse God, and die.

But he said unto her, Thou speakest as one of the foolish women speaketh. What? shall we receive good at the hand of God, and shall we not receive evil? In all this did not Job sin with his lips.

THE BOOK OF JOB 1:21; 2:7-10

I DID not find the world desolate when I entered it; my fathers planted for me before I was born: so do I plant for those who come after me.

TALMUD: *Ta'anith*

*A*T ONE, man is a king, adored by all; at two, he is like a pig, wallowing in dirt; at ten, he skips like a goat; at twenty, he neighs like a horse; married, he works like an ass; when a father, he snarls like a dog; and when old, he dodders like an ape.

MIDRASH: *Ecclesiastes Rabbah, i:2*

A BOOK may be as great a thing as a battle.

BENJAMIN DISRAELI

*W*HO CARRIES butter on his head
should not walk in the sun.

YIDDISH PROVERB

*S*ET ME as a seal upon thine heart, as a
seal upon thine arm: for love is strong as
death; jealousy is cruel as the grave: the
coals thereof are coals of fire, which hath a
most vehement flame.
Many waters cannot quench love, neither
can the floods drown it: if a man would
give all the substance of his house for love,
it would utterly be contemned.

SONG OF SOLOMON 8:6–7

*O*NE OF the most endearing customs I
know involved a Jewish boy's first day at
Hebrew school, or *cheder*.

The teacher would show the boy the
alphabet, on a large chart, and before
(or after) he repeated the teacher's
'aleph' a drop of honey was placed on
his tongue.

'How does that taste?' the boy would
be asked.
'Sweet.'
'The study of the holy Law,' was the
answer, 'is sweeter.'

Sometimes the boy's mother would give
him honeycakes, shaped in the letters of
the alphabet, before he went off to the
cheder on his first day, or when he
returned, to make him know and
remember that 'learning is sweet.'

LEO ROSTEN: *The Joys of Yiddish*

To ACCEPT tradition without examining it with intelligence and judgement, is like the blind blindly following others.

BAHYA IBN PAQUDA: *Duties of the Heart*

When ONE dog barks, he easily finds others to bark with it.

MIDRASH: *Exodus Rabbah 31:9*

Be THE master of your will and the slave of your conscience.

CHASIDIC SAYING

✿ 23 ✿

$\mathcal{E}$VERYONE is commanded to love all human beings as one loves oneself, provided they are good and upright, but one must hate an evil person who will not accept rebuke. One is obliged to love strangers and look after orphans and widows even though they be very wealthy. Anyone who vexes them or provokes them to anger or grieves them or domineers over them or wastes their fortune transgresses a negative precept; this applies much more if one smite them or abuse them or curse them. All this applies when one afflicts them for his own advantage, but if it be for their benefit, e.g., to teach the orphans the Torah[1] or a trade or to train them in the right path, it is permitted. Nevertheless, one must lead them with love and mercy. They are considered to be orphans in that they no longer need the assistance of another and are able to keep themselves. One must not put a stumbling block in the way of a person who is ignorant of the good and righteous way, lest he transgress the Law.

LAWS AND CUSTOMS OF ISRAEL

Torah: the first five books of The Old Testament.

For the commandment is a lamp; and
the law is light; and reproofs of instruction
are the way of life:
To keep thee from evil the woman,
from the flattery of the tongue of a
strange woman.
Lust not after her beauty in thine heart;
neither let her take thee with her eyelids.
For by means of a whorish woman a man
is brought to a piece of bread: and an
adulteress will hunt for the precious life.
Can a man take fire in his bosom, and his
clothes not be burned?
Can one go upon hot coals, and his feet
not be burned?
So he that goeth into his neighbour's wife;
whosoever toucheth her shall not
be innocent…

But whoso committeth adultery with a
woman lacketh understanding; he that
doeth it destroyeth his own soul.
A wound and dishonour shall he get; and
his reproach shall not be wiped away.
For jealousy is the rage of a man; therefore
he will not spare in the day of vengeance.
He will not regard any ransome; neither
will he rest content, though thou
givest many gifts.

PROVERBS 6:23–29; 32–35

To EVERY thing there is a season, and a time to every purpose under the heaven:

A time to be born, and a time to die; a time to plant, and a time to pluck up that which is planted;

A time to kill, and a time to heal; a time to break down, and a time to build up;

A time to weep, and a time to laugh; a time to mourn, and a time to dance;

A time to cast away stones, and a time to gather stones together; a time to embrace, and a time to refrain from embracing;

A time to get, and a time to lose; a time to keep, and a time to cast away;

A time to rend, and a time to sew; a time to keep silence, and a time to speak;

A time to love, and a time to hate; a time of war and a time of peace.

What profit hath he that worketh in
that wherein he laboureth?

I have seen the travail, which God
hath given to the sons of men to be
exercised in it.

He hath made every thing beautiful
in his time: also he hath set the world in
their heart, so that no man can find out the
work that God maketh from the
beginning to the end.

I know that there is no good in them,
but for a man to rejoice, and to do
good all his life.

THE BOOK OF ECCLESIASTES 3:1–12

WHEN THE weasel and the cat make a
marriage, it is a very ill presage.

HEBREW PROVERB

MEN LIKE the opinions to which
they have become accustomed from their
youth; they defend them and shun contrary
views: and this is one of the things that
prevents men from finding the truth, for
they cling to the opinions of habit.

MAIMONIDES: *Guide for the Perplexed*

ANOTHER'S CARES will not
rob you of sleep.

YIDDISH PROVERB

*H*ISTORY TEACHES us that men and
nations behave wisely once they have
exhausted all other alternatives.

ABBA EBAN

*W*E ARE all afraid – for our confidence,
for the future, for the world. That is the
nature of the human imagination. Yet
every man, every civilization, has gone
forward because of its engagement with
what it has set itself to do. The personal
commitment and the emotional
commitment working together as one,
has made the Ascent of Man.

JACOB BRONOWSKI

O DEATH, how bitter is the remembrance of thee to a man that liveth at rest in his possessions, unto the man that hath nothing to vex him, and that hath prosperity in all things: yea, unto him that is yet able to receive meat!

O death, acceptable is thy sentence unto the needy, and unto him whose strength faileth, that is now in the last age, and is vexed with all things, and to him that despaireth, and hath lost patience.

Fear not the sentence of death, remember them that have been before thee, and that come after; for this is the sentence of the Lord over all flesh.

BEN SIRACH: *Apocrypha*
(Ecclesiasticus 41:1–3)

MIRACLES SOMETIMES occur, but one has to work terribly hard for them.

CHAIM WEIZMANN

SOME CAN find money for mischief when they can find none to buy corn.

HEBREW PROVERB

IN MY own city my good name procures respect, in a strange city my clothes do.

BEN SYRA

*T*HE WAY of a fool is right in his own eyes: but he that hearkeneth unto counsel is wise.

A fool's wrath is presently known: but a prudent man covereth shame.

He that speaketh truth sheweth forth righteousness: but a false witness deceit.

There is that speaketh like the piercings of a sword: but the tongue of the wise is health.

PROVERBS 12:15–18

*M*AKE HASTE when you purchase a field; be slow when you marry a wife.

HEBREW PROVERB

*J*HE MORE flesh, the more worms.
The more possessions, the more worry.
The more wives, the more witchcraft.
The more maidservants, the
more unchastity.
The more slaves, the more robbery.
The more Torah, the more life.
The more the company of scholars,
the more wisdom.
The more counsel, the more
understanding.
The more charity the more peace.
If one acquires a good name he acquires
something for himself.
If one acquires for himself knowledge
of the Torah he acquires for himself
life in the world.

HILLEL: *Pirke Abot*

*D*O NOT speak of secret matters in a field full of little hills.

HEBREW PROVERB

*O*NLY OUR concept of time makes it possible for us to speak of the Day of Judgment by that name; in reality it is a summary court in perpetual session.

FRANZ KAFKA

*B*E OF exceedingly humble spirit, for the end of man is the worm.

TALMUD: *Pirke Abot*

*B*LESSED IS he that considereth the poor:
the Lord will deliver him in time
of trouble.

PSALM 41:1

... *U*NLESS THERE is a chance of winning,
it is worse than useless – it is self-defeating
– to react violently to whatever unbearable
conditions an adversary imposes; it is
suicidal to allow oneself to be provoked
to violent reactions against an enemy,
however insufferable his exactions,
unless he can be defeated.

RABBI JOCHANAAN

HE THAT hides hatred with lying lips and
that utters slander is a fool.

PROVERBS 10:18

MAN RUNS towards the grave,
And rivers hasten to the great deep.
The end of all living is their death,
And the palace in time becomes a heap.
Nothing is further than the day gone by,
And nothing nearer than the day to come,
And both are far, far away
from the man hidden in the heart
of the tomb.

SAMUEL HA-NAGID
Trans David Goldstein

Every author should weigh his
work and ask, 'Will humanity gain
any benefit from it?'

NACHMAN OF BRATSLAV

Choose rather to be the tail of lions
than the head of foxes.

HEBREW PROVERB

Moses did not make religion a part
of virtue: but he declared other virtues to
be a part of religion – I mean justice,
fortitude and temperance, and a universal
agreement of the members of the
community with one another.

FLAVIUS JOSEPHUS

Surely human affairs would be far
happier if the power in men to be silent
were the same as that to speak. But
experience more than sufficiently teaches
that men govern nothing with more
difficulty than their tongues.

BARUCH SPINOZA

❧❧

Tread upon thorns while the shoe
is on your foot.

HEBREW PROVERB

❧❧

Happiness is beneficial for the body,
but it is grief that develops the power
of the mind.

MARCEL PROUST

WHEN YOU betray someone else you also betray yourself.

ISAAC BASHEVIS SINGER

🐦 🐦

FOR THE ignorant, old age is as winter; for the learned, it is a harvest.

CHASIDIC SAYING

🐦 🐦

AS LONG as light comes from the great, the light of the lesser is unseen; once the light of the great disappears, the light of the lesser shines.

MIDRASH: *Deuteronomy Rabbah, 5*

*M*EN WORRY over the loss of their possessions but not over the loss of their years – which never return.

*T*HE ANCIENT Jewish people gave the New World a vision of eternal peace, of universal disarmament, of abolishing the teaching and learning of war.

MENACHEM BEGIN

*W*HAT ONE Christian does is his own responsibility, what one Jew does is thrown back at all Jews.

ANNE FRANK

*H*E WHO has a wide mouth has
a narrow heart.

FOLK SAYING

*I*T MAY EASILY come to pass that a vain
man may become proud and imagine
himself pleasing to all when he is in
reality a universal nuisance.

BARUCH SPINOZA

*H*E WHO flees from God flees
into himself.

PHILO

*I*F OUR sense of who we are depends
upon popularity and other people's
opinions of us, we will always be
dependent on those other people. On any
day they have the power to pull the rug
from under us…

Our souls are not hungry for fame,
comfort, wealth or power. Those rewards
create as many problems as they solve…

What frustrates us and robs our lives of joy
is absence of meaning. We may have all the
things on our wish list and still feel empty.
We may have reached the top of our
professions and still feel that something is
missing. We may know that friends and
acquaintances envy us and still feel the
absence of true contentment in our lives.

If we have never known an alternative,
then we assume that the way we are living,
with all of its frustrations, is the only
way to live.

I suspect that the happiest people you know are the ones who work at being kind, helpful and reliable – and happiness sneaks into their lives while they are busy doing those things. It is a by-product, never a primary goal.

The need for meaning is not a biological need, like the need for acceptance and self-esteem. It is a religious need. An ultimate thirst of our souls.

…the life of uninterrupted fun is only a way of escaping from the challenge of doing something significant with…life. Having fun can be the spice of life but it's not its main course, because, when it is over, *nothing* of lasting value remains.

RABBI HAROLD S KUSHNER

☆ 45 ☆

AND THE effect of righteousness
shall be peace;
and the effect of righteousness quietness
and an assurance for ever.

ISAIAH 32:17

I NEVER met a man in whom I failed to
recognize some quality superior to myself;
if he was older, I said he has done more
good than I; if he was younger, I said he
has sinned less; if richer, I said he has given
more to charity; if poorer, I said he has
suffered more; if wiser, I paid honour to
his wisdom; if not wiser, I judged his faults
less severely. Take this to heart, my son.

THE TESTAMENT OF JUDAH
BEN JEHIEL ASHER

A HOUSE testifies that there was a builder, a dress that there was a weaver, a door that there was a carpenter; so our World by its existence proclaims its Creator, God.

adapted from RABBI AKIBA, MIDRASH TEMURA, CH 3

*T*HE DAY is short and the work is much.

SEPHARDIC SAYING

*A*S IS the garden such is the gardener.

HEBREW SAYING

ACKNOWLEDGEMENTS

Pp. 15, 25, 30, 33, 34, 39, 40, 41, 42, 47: *A Handbook of Proverbs*, Henry G Bonn, Bonn Publishing, 1855.

Pp. 13, 19: *The Laws and Customs of Israel*, trans. by G Friedlander, P Vallentine & Sons.

Pp. 40, 43: *Spinoza's Ethics*, J M Dent and E P Dutton, 1910.

P. 14: *East River*, Macdonald & Co. Ltd., 1948.

Pp. 12, 16, 17, 18, 21, 23, 26, 27, 28, 29, 34, 37, 38, 46: Extracts from the Authorized Version of the Bible (The King James Bible), the rights in which are invested in the Crown, are reproduced by permission of the Crown's Patentee, Cambridge University Press.

P. 39: *The Complete Works of Josephus*, The London Printing and Publishing Co.

P. 32: Extracts from *The Apocrypha* are reproduced by permission of Cambridge University Press.

Pp. 20, 31, 33: *The Chambers Book of Quotations*, Robert I Fitzhenry, Chambers Harrap, 1990.

Pp. 15, 23, 30: Reproduced with the permission of Simon & Schuster, Inc., from *A World Treasury of Proverbs*, David Davidoff. Originally published by Cassell & Co., Ltd.

Pp. 36, 40, 41, 42: *The Dictionary of Quotations*, Geddes & Grosset (Pocket Reference Series), 1992.

Pp. 11, 15, 22, 25, 30, 37, 39, 41, 46: *Treasury of Jewish Quotations*, Leo Rosten, reprinted by permission of the publisher, Jason Aronson Inc., Northvale, NJ © 1988.

Pp. 44–5: *When All You've Ever Wanted Isn't Enough*, Rabbi Harold S Kushner, Macmillan, 1987.

P. 24: *The Joys of Yiddish*, Leo Rosten, Virgin Publishing, 1971.

Pp. 11, 15, 20, 22, 35, 47: *The Living Talmud*, Judah Goldin.

P. 31: *The Ascent of Man*, Jacob Bronowski, BBC Books, 1973.

Whilst every effort has been made to secure permission to reproduce material protected by copyright, if there are any omissions or oversights the editor and publisher apologize and will make suitable acknowledgement in future printings of this book